# SURVIVORS OF BEECHING

## John Jackson

AMBERLEY

First published 2018

Amberley Publishing
The Hill, Stroud
Gloucestershire, GL5 4EP

www.amberley-books.com

Copyright © John Jackson, 2018

The right of John Jackson to be identified as
the Author of this work has been asserted in
accordance with the Copyrights, Designs and
Patents Act 1988.

ISBN 978 1 4456 7656 2 (print)
ISBN 978 1 4456 7657 9 (ebook)

British Library Cataloguing in Publication Data.
A catalogue record for this book is available from
the British Library.

Origination by Amberley Publishing.
Printed in the UK.

# What is a Villain?

Who is your favourite villain? Perhaps it's an infamous criminal from a bygone age or a likeable rogue like Macavity, the notorious cat in T. S. Eliot's poem who was brought to life by Andrew Lloyd Webber in his musical *Cats*. For many railway lovers, however, another villain emerged in the 1960s and, unlike Macavity, he would leave a trace of his actions long after he had gone.

Richard Beeching, or Baron Beeching as he was to become, was an engineer who had steadily climbed the ranks within Imperial Chemical Industries (ICI) since joining the company after the Second World War. In the early 1960s the British Transport Commission was replaced by the British Railways Board. In 1961, it was announced in Parliament that its new chairman would be Richard Beeching.

One of the key political issues of the day was the question of how to stem the huge losses occurring on our (nationalised) railways. A considerable loss of more than £40 million had been incurred in 1960 alone. Beeching was the man charged with providing an early solution to this problem, which was no mean feat.

Beeching's team's initial research suggested that:

1. 30 per cent of route miles carried just 1 per cent of passenger and freight.
2. Half of all stations contributed just 2 per cent of total income.

In early 1963, he delivered the first of two reports entitled 'The Reshaping of Britain's Railways'. His plans were sweeping and hugely controversial. Stretching to over 100 pages, the report made several key recommendations that can be summarised:

1. The closure of 7,000 stations (around a third of the UK total).
2. Complete withdrawal of passenger services across 5,000 route miles.
3. The loss of around 70,000 jobs in the railway industry in the short term.
4. A substantial cull of the UK wagon fleet (a total fleet of around 750,000 at the time) – and emphasis on block trains and containers rather than individual wagonloads.

This report was delivered against a backdrop of our railways being regarded, by politicians of both political parties, as an outdated mode of transport and set in a world where their relevance was quickly being replaced by cars and lorries. The then Minister of Transport, Ernest Marples, was known to favour mass closures and Beeching's research provided the necessary evidence to support this approach.

Let's not forget that prior to Beeching, though, we had seen ongoing changes to our rail network. The 1955 Modernisation Plan had seen the rapid switch from steam to diesel and electric power. On nationalisation of the railways in 1948 the workforce stood at around two thirds of a million and the wagon fleet at around 1.2 million. At the time of Beeching's appointment, the workforce had already been reduced to less than half a million, the wagon fleet stood at around 850,000 and 3,000 route miles of passenger railway had already been closed in just over a decade.

Of course, the planned closures were driven by the need to reverse the huge losses being incurred across the rail network and took minimal account of the social impact that would result. Buses were proposed as the cheaper alternative, but in many cases the 'replacements' were either inconvenient for the public to use or, worse, the promised services were not implemented at all. Nevertheless, the report was adopted by the then Conservative government and implementation commenced despite a backlash from the trade unions and, more generally, the public at large.

It's often forgotten that Beeching had no powers to actually close railway lines or stations, merely to put forward the financial case for such recommendations. It would then be for the politicians themselves to decide if a particular line or station had a deserving enough social case for retention.

In October 1964, Britain elected a Labour government, ending over a decade of Tory rule. During the electioneering, the Labour Party pledged to halt the closure process if they were to be elected. This was a pledge on which they quietly backtracked, and on which they didn't deliver.

A few months after the election, Beeching produced his second report, 'The Development of the Major Railway Trunk Links'. It highlighted one of the legacies that had been evident since the early days of our railways. In the nineteenth century, many different companies had competed to build their own railways and this had resulted in large-scale duplication where, as a nationalised railway, more than one line served the same two points.

Beeching estimated that between half and two thirds of the remaining 7,500 route miles fell into this category and that future investment should be restricted to around 3,000 miles only. Inevitably, these recommendations were controversial. Scotland's railways would be reduced to virtually just the Central Belt. Wales would fair only a little better with just the Great Western Main Line as far as Swansea included.

There were examples in England, too. It was envisaged that the East Coast Main Line would terminate at Newcastle, with closure north of there. The Midland Main Line south of Leicester did not feature in his strategic plans.

On the other hand, some lines that were consigned to the 'Beeching Axe' have remained high profile – the Great Central north of Aylesbury, the 'Waverley' route from Carlisle to Edinburgh, the main line from Derby to Manchester through the Peak District and the much-loved Somerset & Dorset to name just a few.

By June 1965, Richard Beeching was back at his desk at ICI. The 'villain' had left his mark on our railway history. It is claimed he said of his actions that his work was 'surgery and not mad chopping'.

Since that time, much has been made of the 'what if' scenarios of 'had this line been saved' or 'had that station remained open'. It was inevitable that a broad-brush approach would be needed given the short time frame between Beeching's appointment, his recommendations and their implementation – and his departure.

Nevertheless, this book takes a look at some of the railway network that has survived, not in the fantasies of the minds of enthusiasts or local campaigners, but in reality. Its contents can broadly be summarised in three sections:

1. Passenger lines that, for whatever reason, escaped closure in the 1960s.
2. Lines closed that have since reopened in full, or in part.
3. Individual stations that were closed and have subsequently reopened.

To many, the freedom offered by private cars has resulted in today's railways having no relevance in their modern lives. Indeed, in some parts of the country not one, but two generations have grown up with no locally accessible rail service. The demographics of our country have also changed considerably, but it is a shame that keeping our rail network in line with such changes has not been part of the planning process.

I can think of no better example than the creation of the 'new' city of Milton Keynes. In 1967, the new town was conceived. It was to receive a new station, Milton Keynes Central, but with access only from north to south and to London in particular. Despite the area's population swelling from around 50,000 in the early 1960s to around a quarter of a million today, it boasts no east to west rail service. Indeed, the main east to west route that passed just to the south of the city, linking Oxford to Cambridge, closed around this time. Although not actually listed within the main Beeching Plan, closure had been proposed a decade earlier and was only narrowly averted.

The long called for reopening of the so-called Varsity Line between the university cities and an offshoot heading west to Aylesbury are still only on the distant horizon. The cost of reopening is made more prohibitive because of the short-sighted selling off of the trackbed, particularly at the eastern end of this route. I often wonder whether I will see passenger services on these routes in my lifetime. The short, 16-mile section of this route – that between Bletchley and Bedford – is but one survivor to be found in the pages that follow.

My wife and I are fortunate enough to be regular rail travellers on today's branch lines across the county of Cornwall. Some of these lines are also featured in this book. They were the fortunate survivors and none more so than the short branch from St Erth to St Ives. The traffic problems in this seaside treasure are well documented and, thankfully, today's railway is playing a part in helping out. Any traveller using the park-and-ride facility on this branch line can not only avoid this road traffic chaos, but will be rewarded with some breathtaking views of our Cornish coastline and beaches before arriving at the seaside. The journey from the West of England Main Line at St Erth down the branch to St Ives may be only 4 miles and take around a quarter of an hour, but every time we travel along it we are reminded of the role the railways can play in the UK's integrated transport structure.

And, as a regular user of the Settle & Carlisle line for almost half a century, I can't imagine a rail network without the breathtaking views that travelling on this line commands. In the 1980s the line's focus was on the spectacular Ribblehead Viaduct, and just what level of government spending was needed to avert the line's closure. It's hard to believe that it was a declared Thatcherite, Michael Portillo, who, as Minister for Transport, became the line's saviour.

Moving a little further north, any reader of my earlier Amberley material will know that Madge Elliot is one of my heroines. If I could single out one person to typify the fight against the 'Beeching Axe' it would be this modest lady from the Scottish Borders. If you've not heard her name before, that is a shame. She may have lost the fight to save the Waverley route from closure, but she continued her battle for almost half a century. She was rewarded by 'her line' being reopened in part, as the Borders Railway, from Edinburgh as far as Tweedbank in 2015.

The line had previously served Newcraighall, some 5 miles out of Edinburgh, but it was the 'new' railway covering the 30 or so miles beyond there that was far more significant. The BBC coverage of the reopening described it as the 'longest domestic railway to be built in the UK in more than 100 years'. It is a fitting tribute that Freightliner's Class 66 locomotive No. 66528 proudly carries Madge Eliot's name.

Several stations along this Borders route are just some of those on a list of stations, now exceeding 150, that have reopened over the last half century. Given the numbers involved, space precludes a mention of all of them here, but examples from across the UK are included towards the end of this book. I am privileged to have visited most, if not all, of these stations on my travels.

Let's not forget the UK has evolved considerably in the half century since Beeching, particularly with regard to the demands of today's population. In many cases, these changing population demands are the underlying reasons for lines and stations being reopened.

I hope you enjoy your journey through these pages as much as I have enjoyed compiling them.

John Jackson

**Fighting for our Railways – Leeds to Settle & Carlisle**

There can be no better example in England of a railway line that galvanised the pro-rail lobby to battle with 'the Establishment' – and win. Suffice is to say that, despite the threat hanging over it for three decades, scenes like this are, thankfully, still to be enjoyed. On 28 June 1997, Nos 37667 *Meldon Quarry Centenary* and 47710 pause at Appleby for the hundreds of passengers and enthusiasts to capture the moment.

**Fighting for our Railways – Scottish Borders Railway**

Sadly, this Scottish battle had to be lost, and the 'Waverley' route closed, before the fight was eventually won – at least in part. The line from Edinburgh to Tweedbank reopened in 2015. On 4 October 2017, a Scotrail Class 158 unit is seen between Stow and Galashiels in typical Scottish Borders scenery.

### Lines Reprieved – St Erth to St Ives (Cornwall)

The 4-mile branch line linking St Erth on the Great Western Main Line was listed for closure but was reprieved just weeks before closure by the Minister for Transport. On 29 May 2017, No. 150101 waits in the branch line platform at St Erth for its next journey along the St Ives Bay line.

Services on the branch are usually formed of a pair of two-car diesel units, particularly at busy times. On 31 May 2016, however, single-car unit No. 153369 is seen arriving at St Erth. Despite being the busy spring Bank Holiday week, this service is short, being formed of three carriages on that day.

The proximity of the line to the Cornish Coast is evident in this view on 31 May 2013. Unit No. 150265 leads a four-car service on the approach to St Ives station. The single-track branch line is worked on a broadly half-hourly service throughout the day. There are no passing loops or sidings to increase capacity, which is further restricted by the platform lengths.

On 31 May 2013, with No. 150261 in the foreground, the four-car set occupies the full platform length. This view is looking towards the town beyond the buffers, with Porthminster beach only a few yards below, to the right.

### Lines Reprieved – Liskeard to Looe

Another Cornish branch line that was scheduled to close was the branch from the Great Western Main Line at Liskeard serving the coastal resort of Looe and intermediate wayside halts. Indeed, it was only reprieved at the very last minute, within weeks of closure. On 27 May 2014, No. 150243 waits in the Looe branch line platform at Liskeard.

The unit above leaves Liskeard seemingly heading in totally the wrong direction as Looe is broadly behind the camera some 9 miles away. The unit reverses at Coombe Junction where, as seen here on 30 May 2016, the train staff are responsible for changing the points to enable the train to proceed.

The branch beyond leads to Moorswater and a cement distribution point served by one of Cornwall's few surviving freight services. On 31 May 2017, Colas-operated No. 70815 waits on the curve at Liskeard on its working from Aberthaw in South Wales. It will trip to Moorswater by working around the passenger unit that uses the single-track branch line in the foreground.

On 31 May 2017, unit No. 153368 is working the branch services. With the town occupying both banks of the river beyond, it waits in Looe's single platform to return to Liskeard. The sidings and a small shed here were removed half a century ago. On a weekday, the unit makes twelve return trips along the branch.

**Lines Reprieved – Plymouth to Gunnislake**

Although the line beyond Gunnislake to Callington was a victim of the Beeching closures, the 14-mile stretch from Plymouth to Gunnislake was reprieved, chiefly because of the poor road alternatives in the area. On 29 May 2014, No. 150106 sits in the western bay platform at Plymouth, waiting to work to Gunnislake.

The Gunnislake branch leaves the Great Western Main Line at St Budeaux for the remaining 11 miles to Gunnislake, including reversal at Bere Alston. Here, on 30 May 2016, single-car No. 153373 is working the service. The crew are in the process of changing ends before proceeding towards Calstock and Gunnislake.

The line skirts the River Tamar for much of its journey, earning it the name of 'The Tamar Valley Line'. On 30 May 2017, No. 150120 is seen at Gunnisake, waiting to form the 13.45 service to Plymouth. The current weekday service consists of nine return trips a day, operating roughly every two hours each way.

On 27 May 2015, it's the turn of No. 150127 to be working on the branch. It is seen shortly after arrival at Gunnislake's single platform.

### Lines Reprieved – Exeter to Exmouth

This Devon branch won a closure reprieve not once, but twice, with closure notice posted in both 1964 and 1967. Nevertheless, the Avocet Line, as it became known, survives – and thrives. On 15 July 2015, No. 150124 arrives at Exeter St Davids with a service from Exmouth, which, on arrival, will reverse and continue as a through service to Paignton.

The city centre of Exeter is better served by its Central station. On 19 November 2015, No. 150101 is calling on a service from Exmouth. The branch diverges from the line to Yeovil Junction a mile or so east of here, at Exmouth Junction. From Exmouth Junction the line to Exmouth itself is a single-track branch of just under 10 miles, with a passing loop at Topsham.

The branch enjoys a service of around thirty trains each way on weekdays and they are timetabled to pass at Topsham station loop. On 1 June 2016, three Class 153 units, Nos 153370, 153382 and 153325, are seen entering the platform loop.

On 1 June 2013, No. 143620 leads a four-car working as it terminates at Exmouth. It will shortly return to Paignton via Exeter. At one time there were no fewer than six platforms at Exmouth station; today, it is a single-platform terminus.

**Lines Reprieved – Ryde to Shanklin**

The Isle of Wight was once served by over 50 miles of railway lines. Under the Beeching proposals, the island would have been left with no rail services at all. This line was the only one on the island reprieved, on the grounds that to go without would cause severe hardship, and this line was electrified instead. On 15 July 2014, No. 483006 crosses the causeway as it heads to Ryde's Pier Head station.

These units are former London Underground coaches and are maintained by the island's facility at Ryde St Johns. On 3 October 2015, unit No. 483002 *Raptor* is stabled on the depot.

The 8-mile branch line that survives has its southern terminus at Shanklin. On 3 October 2015, No. 483007 has just arrived at the single-platform terminus, prior to returning to Pier Head station at Ryde. Today, the Island Line enjoys a twice-an-hour service frequency on weekdays.

The station at Ryde Esplanade is close to the seafront and is most conveniently situated for the majority of the town's amenities. On 3 October 2015, No. 483004 approaches the station on a working to Pier Head.

## Lines Reprieved – Around London

The majority of lines in the London area escaped the sweeping cuts proposed. Greenford's connection to London Paddington via West Ealing was one short branch proposed for closure under the Reshaping Plan, but it was subsequently reprieved. The service has recently changed to a shuttle from Greenford to West Ealing for a connection into the capital. On 16 June 2015, prior to these changes, No. 165136 calls at Ealing Broadway on a through service from Greenford to Paddington.

The lines around Greenford are also served by a daily Chiltern Railways working to and from South Ruislip into London's Paddington station. On 1 September 2016, No. 165028 is seen waiting to leave Paddington on this service.

The 6-mile branch from Watford Junction to St Albans Abbey was reprieved in the 1960s due to a strong voice from local protesters. It has lived in the shadow of closure ever since. Services operate on a single-track, one-engine-on-the-line basis with a broadly 45-minute frequency in each direction. A Class 319 unit operates the service, and on 9 November 2016 No. 319441 was working the Abbey Line – or the 'Abbey Flyer' as it is known locally.

Perhaps the most unlikely series of events affects the Kensington Olympia to Clapham Junction service. In the 1960s just two trains a day each way operated, affectionately known as the 'Kenny Belle'. This service was, perhaps not surprisingly, proposed for closure. The workings did not even appear in the national timetable. I remember as a young lad the look of astonishment I was given by the ticket office at Clapham when I asked for a ticket to Kensington Olympia. I believe this was also the last steam-operated service in the London area. Today, by total contrast, the busy service on this route sees over 100 trains a day operated by both Southern and London Overground, including No. 378144, seen arriving at Clapham on a service from Willesden Junction on 27 April 2017.

### Lines Reprieved – Whitland to Pembroke Dock

Although not included in the original list of proposed closures, this 27-mile-long branch was added later in the 1960s and did not form part of the network for future development. Nevertheless, it survived and enjoys a service running every two hours each way, mostly through to Carmarthen or Swansea. On 11 November 2017, No. 150285 waits at the Pembroke Dock terminus to form the 15.09 service to Swansea.

Today's timetable makes provision for trains to pass at Tenby station. On 11 November 2017, No. 150285, heading west for Pembroke Dock, meets No. 158840, which is heading east to Swansea.

### Lines Reprieved – Shrewsbury to Swansea (via Llandovery)

Perhaps one of the most remarkable survivors is the service on the 'Heart of Wales' line, although cynics might point out it did run through several marginal political constituencies. On 15 July 2015, No. 153303 arrives at its destination of Cardiff Central, having departed Shrewsbury a little over five hours earlier.

The lengthy single-track branch line has several passing loops and the four or five trains each way a weekday pass at either Llandovery or Llanwrtyd. Journeys today also involve reversal at Llanelli, and at Swansea on services continuing to Cardiff. A reduced Sunday service also operates and on 12 November 2017, a Sunday, No. 150240 is seen reversing at Llanelli while working the 11.32 service to Shrewsbury.

**Lines Reprieved – Bletchley to Bedford**

The majority of the 75 miles of the Varsity Line linking Oxford to Cambridge was closed in 1967. The better, faster services via London were offered as the preferred alternative, although this was a journey of 120 miles. The exception was the 16-mile stretch linking Bletchley to Bedford, which was reprieved. On 19 July 2016, No. 150105 arrives at Bletchley.

The Marston Vale line serves eleven local stations as well as the main line stations at Bletchley and Bedford. On 12 November 2016, No. 153356 calls at Stewartby on a service to Bedford.

Sixteen trains operate in each direction on weekdays, with the line being double-tracked for most of its length. On 8 November 2016, No. 150109 waits to leave Bedford on the single-track section 'round the corner' to St Johns station, from where it will soon reach the double-tracked branch.

The line provides a useful connection between the Midland to West Coast main lines. It also sees occasional freight traffic, such as No. 66614, seen here on 14 April 2018. It is passing Ridgmont with returning empties from Bletchley to Barrow Hill sidings, near Chesterfield.

### Lines Reprieved – Derby to Matlock

One of the more controversial closures saw the withdrawal of services on the former Midland Main Line from Manchester to London via the Derbyshire Peak District. Both Beeching and Barbara Castle, Minster for Transport in the mid-1960s, held sway over the line's future. The result was the line between Matlock and Chinley closing completely, leaving Matlock being served by a branch line south to Derby. On 21 July 2016, two single-car units, Nos 153357 and 153374, wait at Matlock to form a service to Newark Castle.

The line is now single track from Matlock to Ambergate Junction. Matlock Bath station is within this single-track section. No. 156413 calls here, also on 21 July 2016.

The 'Derwent Valley Line', the branding under which the line is now marketed, sees broadly an hourly service operating seventeen times each way a day, most running through to Newark Castle. On 22 March 2018, No. 156413 calls at Whatstandwell on a service to Matlock.

On the same day Nos 153311 and 153313 are seen leaving Duffield, again heading towards Matlock. The local service shares the main Derby to Sheffield line tracks between Derby and the junction at Ambergate.

**Lines Reprieved – Boston to Skegness**

In common with many other lines in rural Lincolnshire, withdrawal notices were issued for the line between Firsby and Skegness, with proposed station closures including Skegness itself. Thankfully, that decision was later reversed. On 11 May 2018, No. 158785 waits to leave the seaside terminus with the 13.15 service to Nottingham. All services are operated by East Midlands Trains (EMT).

EMT's Class 156 units are also found on services between Nottingham and Skegness. On the same day, No. 156470 arrives on the next hour's eastbound service.

EMT units cover the 80-mile journey from Nottingham to Skegness in just over two hours. Most units travel via Grantham, where they are required to reverse. On 25 March 2015, No. 156410 is doing so on its way to Skegness.

Network Rail's test trains make occasional visits to the line, which is single track in places. A pair of Class 37s, with No. 37116 leading, prepare to leave Nottingham as they head for Skegness on 11 May 2018, the working timetabled around the line's passenger services.

### Lines Reprieved – Buxton to Manchester

The lines further north in Derbyshire were also earmarked for closure, with perhaps Buxton station's proposed closure being the most significant loss. On 20 March 2018, Nos 150118 and 156440 wait to leave on a service to Manchester.

The town of Buxton was originally served by two stations, both with an overall roof and a shared wall. Today, only the fan window survives. It can be seen in this view taken on 22 March 2018, with No. 156461 in the foreground.

An hourly daytime service operates on the branch from Buxton to Manchester. The intermediate stations have survived, including Dove Holes. On 20 March 2018, No. 150118 passes here after a recent snowfall.

A two-car diesel unit is usually diagrammed, with pairs operating at peak times. On 28 October 2014, No. 156482 waits to leave Manchester Piccadilly on an off-peak service.

**Lines Reprieved – Sheffield to Manchester (via the Hope Valley)**

The alternative route via Woodhead linking the two cities had been recently modernised and offered a quicker route for through passengers. The closure of the line via the Hope Valley was therefore proposed, but the plans were changed after consultation. On 21 March 2018, No. 142048 passes Edale signal box on a stopping service to Sheffield.

On the same day, No. 150269 calls at Hathersage station. Local stations now enjoy an hourly service for most of the day.

Long-distance services also benefit from the line's retention, with both East Midlands Trains and Northern by Arriva offering through workings. On 21 March 2018, No. 156406 passes through Bamford station on a Liverpool to Norwich working. The Class 156 will be removed at Nottingham, leaving the more usual Class 158 (on the rear here) to continue to Norwich.

TransPennine Express operate along the Hope Valley with services between Manchester Airport and Cleethorpes. On 21 March 2018, No. 185111 is seen passing Hathersage, heading east.

**Lines Reprieved – Llandudno to Blaenau Ffestiniog**

The Conwy Valley Line stretches for almost 30 miles following the river of the same name. It continues to enjoy a service of six return trips daily between Llandudno and Blaenau Ffestiniog. On 13 June 2018, No. 150259 waits at the terminus, ready to form the 11.35 service to Llandudno.

Taken just a few minutes earlier, this photograph shows users of the arriving service together with the adjacent platform, home to the Ffestiniog Railway.

On 14 June 2018, No. 150240 skirts the Conwy Estuary while making a request stop at Glan Conwy. This morning service saw one passenger get on and one get off here.

The branch line connects with the main North Wales Coast line at Llandudno Junction. On 14 June 2018, No. 150240 waits to leave the Junction station and head to Llandudno. It had just provided a connection to both east and westbound services.

**Lines Reprieved – Liverpool to Southport**

The electrified line north of the Mersey was on the original 'hit list', but it survived. It is now an important part of the Merseyrail network, with a 15-minute service frequency throughout the day between Southport and Liverpool South Parkway (for the airport). On 27 October 2014, No. 507027 waits at Southport on a southbound service.

Units are outstabled at Southport between duties. On 27 October 2014, No. 507031 awaits its next duty.

The main electric unit servicing depot on the north side of the Mersey is at Kirkdale. Several units are seen here during off-peak hours on 28 October 2015.

Sandhills station enjoys an even more frequent service. As well as the Southport service, Merseyrail trains to both Kirkby and Ormskirk serve here. Unit No. 507018 calls on 18 June 2014.

### Lines Reprieved – Leeds to Ilkley

Another electrified survivor can be found across the Pennines. While services north from Ilkley to Skipton, and the associated spur line to Otley, were victims of closure, this 15-mile branch survived. On 18 May 2017, No. 333014 arrives at Leeds on a service from Ilkley.

Reflecting a remarkable change in fortunes, the lines in Airedale and Wharfedale were electrified in the mid-1990s. Skipton, Ilkley, Bradford and Leeds were duly electrified and Class 333 units became the line's operators. On 23 July 2014, No. 333001 is waiting at Leeds for its time to return to Ilkley.

Four trains an hour operate each way on the branch section between Guiseley and Ilkley. Here, on 30 October 2015, No. 333010 calls at Burley in Wharfedale.

There's not much evidence to show today that Ilkley was once a through station. On 30 October 2015, No. 333014 is seen in the platform at today's terminus.

**Lines Reprieved – Harrogate to York**

Line closures around Harrogate saw towns such as Ripon and Wetherby left with no railway. It is perhaps surprising therefore that the line between Harrogate and York survived, with Knaresborough housing the only population of any size on route. On 19 April 2018, No. 150139 (with No. 153304 on the rear, see below) has just terminated on a service from Leeds.

Single-car units such as No. 153304 are often used to strengthen services on the section between Knaresborough, Harrogate and Leeds in particular. After shunting, No. 153304 will lead the three-car formation on its return to Leeds.

Later the same day, No. 150271 has arrived at Cattal. The driver and signalman are carrying out the token exchange for the single-track section to Knaresborough.

This east–west line gives the people of Harrogate a number of options through changing trains at York station. On 18 May 2016, No. 155342 has just terminated on a working from the town.

**Lines Reprieved – Scarborough to Bridlington and Hull**

The good news was that this section was not initially listed for complete closure. The bad news, however, was the need to later re-examine the case for closing the line. This was after the closure of lines nearby and a resultant drop in passenger numbers and, therefore, revenue. After considerable pruning of tracks and loss-making stations it survived – just. On 17 April 2018, No. 158860 has just terminated at Bridlington on a service from Hull.

Bridlington station is a Grade II listed building. The expanse of the station can be seen in this view of No. 158860. The through lines to Scarborough veer off to the left.

The Scarborough to Bridlington section enjoys nine trains each way on weekdays. On 17 April 2018, No. 158848 leaves Filey on a service to Scarborough. The spur from here to the Holiday Camp station closed in 1977.

A little further south, No. 158844 calls at Driffield on 17 April 2018. Class 158s are the mainstay traction on this line.

**Lines Reprieved – Barrow to Whitehaven**

This stretch of the Cumbrian Coast line covers around 50 miles and chiefly hugs the coastline. The line was listed for closure together with the associated section from Barrow to Carnforth. On 15 June 2018, No. 156491 leaves Drigg on a service from Carlisle to Lancaster via Barrow.

On the same day, No. 156479 skirts the Irish Sea at Sellafield. The town is better known among rail enthusiasts for the Direct Rail Services' workings to and from the BNF plant here.

The operator is also offering Northern by Arriva a helping hand with loco-hauled services complementing their own unit workings, particularly as the line enjoys a much-improved frequency of service today. On 15 June 2018, No. 68017 *Hornet* (with No. 68003 *Astute* on the rear) is seen heading through Foxfield with the 06.16 Carlisle to Barrow.

A single Class 37 is also employed on these coastal workings. On 15 June 2018, No. 37403 *Isle of Mull* propels the 09.19 Carlisle to Barrow away from Ravenglass.

**Lines Reprieved – Middlesbrough to Whitby**

The branch line, marketed under the brand 'Esk Valley Line', is around 35 miles long and follows the River Esk for much of its route. On 16 April 2018, No. 156463 waits at Whitby to work the 15.59 service to Middlesbrough.

Unit No. 156463 arrives at Grosmont. The station area here is shared with the North Yorkshire Moors Railway (NYMR) to the left of this photograph. Northern by Arriva's service of four trains each way, seven days a week since 2017, is complemented by a similar number running through from Grosmont or Pickering using a NYMR first generation diesel multiple unit.

Later in its Middlesbrough-bound journey, No. 156463 has to reverse at the remote outpost of Battersby. The single platform here is all that is required for normal service days. The run round loop is retained for the use of any loco-hauled specials.

On 10 February 2014, No. 156463 approaches journey's end at Middlesbrough after its 90-minute journey from Whitby.

**Lines Reprieved – Ayr to Stranraer**

The more direct line to the English Border from Dumfries to Stranraer was closed in 1965. By contrast, the line, which runs 76 miles from Ayr to the Scottish port, was reprieved, partly to appease politicians and businessmen from Northern Ireland. The sleeper service to the Scottish port offered them a shipping connection to the province and that working lingered on until the early 1990s. On 17 October 2017, No. 156513 crosses the River Ayr on the approach to Ayr station with a service bound for Stranraer.

Many services to and from Stranraer are now extended through to either Carlisle or Kilmarnock. On 17 October 2017, No. 156509 passes an empty Falkland Yard, north of Ayr, on a southbound service.

South of Ayr, the service to Stranraer runs approximately every two hours. It is augmented with additional trains to Maybole and Girvan. On 17 October 2017, No. 156492 has just terminated at Girvan and waits to return to Ayr.

On the same day, No. 156502 calls at Maybole while working from Stranraer to Kilmarnock.

## Lines Reprieved – Fort William to Mallaig

The threat of closure hung over the West Highland Line extension to Mallaig from the time of Beeching through to the 1980s. This is hardly surprising as the line has been a lossmaker since first being built – the only debate is as to how much. On 15 October 2013, No. 156492 waits to leave Mallaig on its 164-mile journey to Glasgow Queen Street.

The line has, of course, been rated one of the most scenic rail journeys in the world. The curved, 400-yard-long viaduct at Glenfinnan is one of the most impressive landmarks on the line, and the line's retention is due in part to its appearance in a number of *Harry Potter* films. On 6 April 2016, No. 156476 is seen crossing the structure.

Scotrail's four daily services on the line are supplemented by the 'Jacobite' steam trains operated by West Coast Railway Company, with two further trains a day. On 12 October 2017, Black 5 No. 45407 waits at Mallaig to work tender-first back to Fort William.

On 15 October 2013, No. 156499 stands at Fort William, waiting to work the 41 miles to Mallaig.

**Lines Reprieved – Inverness to Kyle of Lochalsh**

Another concerted effort was required to keep this Scottish line from closure. It was earmarked in the Beeching Report and remained unloved by British Rail. In the early 1970s the Secretary of State for Transport agreed to its closure, but it won a last-minute reprieve. On 11 October 2017, Nos 158714 and 158722 pass at Dingwall while working Kyle line services.

Four services operate each way on weekdays along this 64-mile-long line. On 11 October 2017, No. 158714 has just arrived at Kyle with the first working of the day from Inverness, at just after 11.30! The Isle of Skye is in the background.

The return working for No. 158714 is scheduled to pass the next westbound service in the passing loop at the remote station outpost of Strathcarron. On this occasion its classmate is No. 158705.

Charter trains are regular visitors to this scenic line. On 4 April 2015, Nos 37607 and 37218 are seen approaching Dingwall on a return charter from Kyle of Lochalsh.

### Lines Reprieved – Inverness to Wick & Thurso

Another Scottish railway battle saw the proposed closure of the Far North Line between Inverness, Wick and Thurso reversed. On 3 April 2015, No. 158724 has just arrived at Inverness with a service from Wick.

On 10 October 2017, No. 158708 waits to leave Inverness on the mid-morning service to Wick via Thurso – a journey of 174 miles in length. Four trains make the full journey each way on weekdays, with additional services serving the southern end of the route.

The rail journey is more circuitous than the road alternative via the A9. On 11 October 2017, No. 158720 arrives at Invergordon around 53 minutes after leaving Inverness for Wick. The rail journey from Inverness to here already measures 31 miles against the road distance of 23 miles.

The remote community of Rogart is just under halfway between Inverness and Wick. On 4 April 2015, No. 158716 arrives at the wayside halt. The 77-mile rail journey from here to Inverness takes exactly two hours. It's hardly a fair contest as the road distance via the A9 is just 53 miles.

**Lines Reopened – Romsey to Eastleigh (via Chandler's Ford)**

In 1969, passenger services were withdrawn from this route and Chandler's Ford station closed. A single-track line was retained for local stone traffic, resulting in a reduction in the cost of reinstating a passenger service in 2003. On 29 April 2017, No. 158887 comes off the branch as it approaches Eastleigh.

The non-electrified line enjoys an hourly service throughout the day, typically using a South Western Railways' Class 158 two-car diesel unit. On 30 April 2017, No. 158885 calls at Chandler's Ford.

The single-platform structure of the rebuilt station at Chandler's Ford can be seen here as No. 158885 leaves for Romsey.

The service now operates from Romsey to Salisbury via Southampton Central. On 30 April 2017, No. 158881 is seen at Eastleigh on a working destined for Salisbury.

**Lines Reopened – Barry to Bridgend (via Llantwit Major)**

This 20-mile section of the 'Vale of Glamorgan' line was closed to passengers in 1964. The trackbed remained intact for freight traffic, in particular to Ford at Bridgend and Aberthaw Power Station. Passenger services were reinstated in 2005. On 10 November 2017, No. 150267 calls at Llantwit Major on a service towards Cardiff.

The line now enjoys an hourly service each way throughout the day, with many services operating to or from Aberdare or Merthyr Tydfil. Arriva Trains Wales operate these services and No. 150267, seen leaving Llantwit Major, will work through to Aberdare.

The case for reopening the line was strengthened by increased traffic using Cardiff International Airport. A station at Rhoose, close to the airport, was incorporated in the plans. On 10 November 2017, a pair of Class 142 units, Nos 142069 and 142010, call at Rhoose station, which now sees a regular bus connection to Cardiff International Airport.

Secondary lines across the UK require help in coping with the Autumn leaf-fall season and the Vale of Glamorgan line is no exception. On the same November day, Nos 66047 and 66117 'top and tail' a typical Rail Head Treatment Train (RHTT), which is seen passing through Llantwit Major.

**Lines Reopened – Ebbw Vale Town to Cardiff**

The purist might argue that this line should not be included here as it had already been condemned to closure a few months before the Beeching Report. Had its fate not already been decided, however, surely it would have fallen victim to the axe. Closed in 1962, the passenger service was reinstated in 2008. On 8 November 2017, No. 142010 calls at Newbridge on a service towards Cardiff.

The line enjoys an hourly weekday service each way between Ebbw Vale Town and Cardiff. One of the line's tireless campaigners for reopening, Peter Law – the Welsh Assembly member for Blaenau in Gwent – had been fighting for decades for reinstatement to Newport (and then onwards to Cardiff), but that was not to be. Newport station is avoided on the train's 60-minute journey to the Welsh capital. On 10 November 2017, No. 150242 arrives at Cardiff while forming a through service from Bridgend to Ebbw Vale Town.

Reopened in 2008, the line stretched around 18 miles from the Great Western Main Line to the then terminus at Ebbw Vale Parkway. The remaining couple of miles was subsequently reopened to Town station in 2015. On 8 November 2017, No. 143602 waits at the terminus to form the 13.37 service to Cardiff Central.

The Ebbw Vale service regularly uses the recently opened Platform 0 at Cardiff Central. On 15 July 2015, No. 150280 is about to leave the platform for Ebbw Vale Town. This photograph was taken about two months after the new terminus was opened.

**Lines Reopened – Bridgend to Maesteg**

The line – part of the route from Bridgend to Treherbert, via Maesteg and Cymmer – saw closure in 1970. By then, the section beyond Maesteg had already been consigned to history, partly due to damage to Cymmer Tunnel, caused by mining subsidence. The Maesteg branch was reopened in 1992. On 10 November 2017, No. 150280 is seen arriving at Maesteg.

Just a few minutes later, No. 150280 is ready to head towards Bridgend and Cardiff on a through working to Cheltenham Spa.

Sister unit No. 150281 is seen here at Tondu, where a passing loop on the single-track branch is provided. The driver is collecting the token from the signalman at the junction signal box as authority to proceed.

With its mission accomplished, the unit is soon on its way northwards towards Maesteg.

### Lines Reopened – Abercynon to Aberdare

The line to Aberdare splits from the branch to Merthyr at Abercynon. This section fell victim to closure and passenger services were withdrawn in 1964. It was to be reopened almost a quarter of a century later, in 1988. On 9 November 2017, No. 150245 calls at Abercynon while working the 14.19 service to Aberdare.

The branch enjoys a half-hourly service for most of the day on weekdays. To maintain this level of service on the single-track branch, the passing loop at Mountain Ash is used. On 9 November 2017, units Nos 150282 and 150250 meet in the loop here.

The branch line had been retained for coal traffic serving Tower Colliery, to the north of Aberdare, thus safeguarding the trackbed. This colliery, closed in 2008, was to be the last deep-coal mine in South Wales. By the time of its closure, the passenger service had of course long been revived. On 9 November 2017, No. 150282 waits at the terminus on a through service to Barry Island.

As can be seen in this shot, the track north of Aberdare towards Tower Colliery remains in place, and talk of extending the passenger service by a further 3 miles to Hirwaun remains a possibility.

### Lines Reopened – Leamington Spa to Coventry

Local services were withdrawn on the line in 1965, when it fell victim to the Beeching Axe. In 1976, however, Birmingham International station opened, and a year later a number of through services were diverted to use the Leamington to Coventry line in order to serve this new station. On 9 May 2018, CrossCountry Voyager No. 220012 calls at Leamington Spa on a service to Manchester Piccadilly.

The same day, No. 221121 heads non-stop through Kenilworth on another Manchester-bound service. The station here had finally reopened a few days earlier.

Kenilworth station is served by an hourly service on weekdays using a single-car Class 153 unit. The unit shuttles between Leamington and Coventry, making seventeen trips a day. On 9 May 2018, No. 153354 is working the service.

Later that day, several passengers are waiting at Coventry to board the same unit as it forms the 15.36 service to Leamington Spa.

### Lines Reopened – Kettering to Corby

The 7 miles between these two Northamptonshire towns have seen an on/off saga spanning thirty years. Closed through the Beeching Report in the 1960s, it was reopened in 1987 but closed again in 1990 after an unsuccessful, or perhaps unreliable, service. Then, in 2009, the station reopened in its latest guise (see below). On 20 May 2016, No. 222011 waits at Corby to work a service to St Pancras.

The service was eventually incorporated into the franchise that is currently operated by East Midlands Trains and services were incorporated into their timetables and operated when new rolling stock arrived in 2009. On 20 May 2016, the usual five-car Meridian, in this case No. 222022, arrives at Corby.

In a remarkable change of fortunes, the line is to see electrification and a half-hourly service frequency between Corby and London. In the interim, one of East Midlands Trains' High Speed Trains, acquired from Grand Central, makes one return trip daily in the transitional timetable. The working is seen approaching Kettering on 7 June 2018 with power car No. 43468 leading.

We may never know how much today's passenger service owes to Corby's steel workings, which run to and from Margam Yard in South Wales. This service has operated through the town's station platforms for many years, safeguarding the trackbed. On 20 May 2016, No. 66094 heads the return empties, bound for Margam, through Corby station.

**Lines Reopened – Coventry to Nuneaton**

The passenger service was withdrawn in January 1965 under the Beeching Report. The line was reopened in 1987 and the rebuilt intermediate station at Bedworth opened a year later. On 16 January 2015, No. 153334 waits at Nuneaton on a Coventry service.

The line is currently served by sixteen trains each way on weekdays, operated by a single London North Western Class 153 unit. On 21 April 2017, No. 153364 arrives at Coventry on a service from Nuneaton.

In 2016, two new stations opened on the line, at Bermuda Park and Coventry Arena. This latter station is approximately half a mile from the Longford & Exhall station, which was closed way back in 1949. As the name suggests, it serves the nearby Ricoh Arena as well as providing a park and ride facility. On 26 June 2017, No. 153371 calls at Coventry Arena on its way to Nuneaton. Perversely, the station is temporarily closed, on safety grounds, around the time of any events starting or ending!

Again, freight traffic using the line safeguarded its retention. On 3 March 2014, No. 66516 is about to thread through Coventry station and take the Nuneaton branch. It is working a Freightliner from Southampton to Trafford Park (Manchester).

**Lines Reopened – Walsall to Rugeley Trent Valley**

'The Chase Line' as it is now known was another 1965 victim of the Beeching closures. It was subsequently reopened, albeit in stages. On 26 February 2015, two-car unit No. 170512 waits at Walsall to head across 'The (Cannock) Chase'.

The 15-mile line now enjoys a half-hourly service throughout the day on weekdays between Rugeley Trent Valley and Birmingham New Street. Indeed, its long-term future is surely secure as it is in the process of being electrified. On 26 February 2015, No. 170508 arrives at Walsall on a service to Birmingham New Street.

The services terminate at Rugeley's Trent Valley station, where connections onto local services along the West Coast Main Line are available. On 18 July 2016, No. 170503 waits in the platform to return to Birmingham, which is just under an hour's journey away.

On the same day, No. 170516 is seen leaving the branch line and approaching Rugeley. In the background is the now-closed power station that, ironically, saw a regular flow of coal traffic along the line while it was closed to passengers.

## Lines Reopened – Spalding to Peterborough

This closure was a short lived one, with the passenger service being withdrawn in 1970. The service was reinstated shortly afterwards, in June 1971, but by then the intermediate stations had closed (without reprieve). On 11 May 2018, No. 153311 arrives at Spalding on a Lincoln to Peterborough service.

On 30 June 2017, No. 153321 waits at Peterborough, about to work the 16.25 service to Lincoln.

Services across Lincolnshire were particularly badly affected by the Beeching closures, despite some lines grimly hanging on into the early 1970s. On 4 July 2015, No. 153311 is seen at Werrington, where the line to Spalding diverges from the East Coast Main Line.

In 1971, the service from Spalding was diverted away from March (on closure of the line) and ran to Peterborough instead. Today, the surviving service runs approximately twelve times each way per weekday, almost all using Platform 1 in Spalding in either direction, as seen here with No. 153376 calling on 7 May 2018.

**Lines Reopened – Nottingham to Mansfield & Worksop**

The 'Robin Hood' line, as it is known today, closed in the 1960s and reverted to a freight-only route for the next forty years or so. It has since been reopened in stages. The section from Nottingham to Newstead came first, in 1993, with intermediate stations at Bulwell and Hucknall. On 22 June 2018, No. 156411 heads north from Hucknall on a service to Worksop.

At Hucknall the station is shared with the Nottingham Tram network, with East Midlands Trains operating services on a single-line basis between here and Bulwell. On 22 June 2018, No. 156408 calls on its way to Nottingham.

The line was extended to Mansfield Woodhouse in 1995. On 12 October 2012, No. 156410 is seen at Mansfield's town station. Services run half-hourly each way between Nottingham and here, with an hourly extension through to Worksop.

On 21 March 2014, No. 156498 waits time at Worksop before returning to Nottingham. The 42-mile journey will take around 75 minutes.

### Lines Reopened – Edinburgh to Tweedbank

This line must surely take pride of place for many reasons. It was closed in January 1969 as part of the infamous 'Waverley' route between Edinburgh and Carlisle. Reopening as far as Tweedbank took place in 2015, under the branding 'Borders Railway'. It was a red-letter day in the life of Madge Eliot (see below). On 4 October 2017, No. 158869 is stabled at Tweedbank waiting its next duty.

The line had closed despite pressure from the newly elected local MP, David Steel, and local housewife Madge Eliot. It is fitting that Freightliner's No. 66528 bears her name. She was relentless in her efforts to see the line reopened despite the fact that, unlike many other lines in this book, the majority of the track had been lifted back in the 1970s. On 4 October 2017, No. 158735 calls at Galashiels.

Despite a number of breaches of the trackbed, over 30 miles of line was rebuilt. Gorebridge was, at one stage, mooted as the potential southern terminus on cost grounds. No. 170460 calls at the station on 4 October 2017. As can be seen, it was not to be the end of the line, which is currently a further 23 miles away, at Tweedbank.

On the same day, No. 158738 is seen in the double-track section near Stow. A broadly half-hourly service operates around thirty times each way a day.

**Lines Reopened – Rutherglen to Whifflet**

The former Rutherglen & Coatbridge Railway was axed in 1966. It reopened in 1993 after rebuilding, with Whifflet, not Coatbridge, as the line's new destination. On 14 May 2014, No. 158869 waits at Whifflet for return to Glasgow Central.

The electrification of the 10-mile line was completed just a few months later. This not only freed up diesel units, but also enabled trains to run half-hourly through Glasgow Central's Low Level platforms. On 16 October 2017, No. 318262 is seen at Whifflet on one such service to Dalmuir.

Class 320 units are also found on these services, as these two shots demonstrate. First, No. 320302 terminates at Whifflet on arrival from Dalmuir on 16 October 2017.

Second, classmate No. 320309 arrives at Kirkwood on a service through to Motherwell on the same day.

## Lines Reopened – Glasgow Central to Paisley Canal

Today's 7-mile branch line to Paisley originally went through to Elderslie, with services later being diverted to Kilmacolm. The 1960s rundown of the line saw Glasgow services terminating at Paisley Canal, and then later at Hawkhead. This section saw freight traffic to the oil terminal there. By 1983 the rundown was complete and the line closed to all passenger traffic. Reopening occurred in 1990. On 14 October 2013, No. 314205 waits at the Paisley terminus to return to Glasgow.

Track lifting in the 1980s meant that the original Canal station could not be accessed, and a new station was built nearer to Glasgow. On 31 March 2015, No. 314204 is seen at the 'new' terminus.

When electrification of the line was being considered, the business case was improved by the part electrification from Shields to Corkerhill to enable electric units to reach the depot there. On 8 April 2015, No. 314204 calls at Corkerhill on a service to Glasgow Central.

Glasgow Central sees services running half-hourly to Paisley Canal from 06.30 to 23.30 on weekdays. The journey time of approximately 20 minutes means the service can be operated by two units throughout the day. On 16 August 2013, No. 314203 has just arrived at Central.

**Lines Reopened – Stirling to Alloa**

Closed in 1968, the 7-mile line was reopened to passenger traffic as far as Alloa in 2008. At the time there was a regular flow of coal traffic to Longannet Power Station, which would benefit from a shorter, more efficient route to the power station. On 7 October 2017, No. 170473 waits to leave Stirling on an 11.01 departure to Alloa.

On the same day, a four-car unit is arriving at Alloa on the 10.10 service from Glasgow Queen Street. No. 156457 is nearest camera in this shot.

With No. 156449 now leading, the pair will form the 10.41 service back to Stirling and Glasgow Queen Street. The line to the left was used to carry coal traffic through to Longannet before the power station's closure.

Just 12 minutes after leaving Alloa, the pair arrive in Stirling. Alloa enjoys an hourly service to Glasgow each weekday, the 36-mile journey taking just under an hour to complete.

**Stations Reopened – Alfreton**

Many of the stations that have been reopened are located on lines covered earlier in this book. On the remaining pages we take a look at a cross-section of reopened stations not covered thus far. For simplicity, they are featured in alphabetical, not geographical, order, starting with Alfreton. Northern unit No. 158849 calls on 13 April 2018 while working a Leeds to Nottingham service.

Closed in 1967, the station was reopened in 1973 as Alfreton and Mansfield Parkway. The town of Mansfield did not have a (closer) station at the time. East Midlands Trains services, also using Class 158s, call on services between Norwich and Liverpool. No. 158862 calls on a Norwich-bound service on 13 April 2018.

### Stations Reopened – Birmingham Snow Hill

Electrification of nearby New Street saw a run down in services from this rival station during the 1960s, resulting in closure in 1972. Demolition soon followed, although reopening came some fifteen years later, with a replacement four-platform station. On 2 October 2013, No. 172214 is seen on a local West Midlands service.

On the same day, No. 67017 waits in Snow Hill station on a Chiltern Railways service.

**Stations Reopened – Clitheroe**

The station's regular rail services were axed in the early 1960s, leaving the line seeing only special Dales-related trains thereafter. Formal reopening happened in 1994. On 14 June 2018, Northern by Arriva's No. 150269 waits in Clitheroe platform.

This unit will form a service from here to Blackburn, along with single car No. 153315, which will lead the three-car rake on its return journey. The line now enjoys an hourly service throughout weekdays.

**Stations Reopened – Coleshill Parkway**

The original station at Coleshill closed in 1968 and reopened as Coleshill Parkway in 2007. On 22 October 2013, No. 170637 calls on an eastbound service towards Leicester.

Although managed by West Midlands Trains, all passenger services are operated by CrossCountry Trains. On 23 February 2017, both Nos 170519 and 170107 were halted here by storm Doris as fallen trees were blocking the line between here and Nuneaton.

**Stations Reopened – Glasgow Central Low Level**

The subterranean platforms here fell victim to the Beeching Act in 1964. By the end of the 1970s, however, their usefulness had been recognised and the platforms were reopened. On 1 April 2015, No. 318267 calls on a North Clyde-bound service to Milngavie.

The reopening gave many advantages, including easing congestion at the main Central station. It also gave the flexibility of through journeys, such as this one, headed by No. 318251 on 16 October 2016. It is arriving at Partick on a service from Milngavie to Cumbernauld.

**Stations Reopened – Ilkeston**

The new station opened in April 2017. It is on the site of the former Ilkeston Junction and Cossall station, which was closed in January 1967. On 22 June 2018, No. 150271 calls on a service from Nottingham to Leeds.

Although several additional East Midlands Trains services have been added in May 2018's timetable changes, Northern operates the majority of services. An hourly service is provided each way for most of the day on weekdays. On 22 June 2018, No. 158859 slows to call on its way to Nottingham.

**Stations Reopened – Llanfairpwll…**

This Anglesey station was closed in 1966 and saw temporary reopening when fire on the Britannia Bridge closed the through line to and from Holyhead in the 1970s. It has since reopened permanently, drawing tourists to its lengthy station signs. More importantly, it offers passengers around twenty services each weekday both towards Holyhead and eastward along the North Wales Coast.

On 13 June 2018, Arriva Trains Wales' No. 158825 calls on a service to Holyhead.

### Stations Reopened – Loch Awe

This Oban line station was another victim of the Beeching Axe in the mid-1960s. It reopened twenty years later. The remote station has a weekday service of six trains each way between Oban and Glasgow. On 13 October 2017, No. 156476 calls on a Glasgow service.

The station's position on the north bank of the loch of the same name can be seen in this view of the same working.

**Stations Reopened – Needham Market**

The original Needham station closed in the mid-1960s. The reopened Suffolk station, now named Needham Market, was opened in the early 1970s. On 8 September 2017, No. 170204 calls on a service to Ipswich.

The majority of services calling here, operated by Greater Anglia, link Ipswich and Cambridge. Each weekday around twenty trains operate in both directions. One of their two-car units, No. 170273, calls on the same day.

**Stations Reopened – Sileby**

This victim of closure in 1968 was to be reopened as part of the 'Ivanhoe' line in the mid-1990s. Further reopenings to serve the likes of Coalville and Ashby-de-la-Zouch have not materialised. On 12 April 2018, No. 156413 calls on a northbound service for Lincoln.

An hourly weekday service between Leicester and Loughborough sees trains calling here, with most extending northwards beyond Nottingham to Lincoln. On the same day, No. 156470 calls at Sileby on a Lincoln to Leicester service.

**Stations Reopened – Tutbury and Hatton**

Tutbury station, on the line between Derby, Stoke-on-Trent and Crewe, closed in 1966. The villages of Tutbury (Staffordshire) and Hatton (Derbyshire) are now served by the reopened station of Tutbury and Hatton. On 22 June 2018, No. 153357 calls on its way to Crewe.

East Midlands Trains operates an hourly weekday service in both directions, usually worked by single-carriage Class 153s. On the same day, No. 153311 heads in the opposition direction, to Derby.

**Stations Reopened – Willington**

The original station, named Repton and Willington, closed under Beeching in the late 1960s. The rebuilt station of Willington opened in the mid-1990s and sees just seven trains each way a day. On 22 June 2018, Nos 170115 and 170117 call on a southbound service.

CrossCountry operate these services on their Nottingham, Derby, Birmingham and Cardiff route. Two-car unit No. 170521 is seen here calling on a service bound for Derby and Nottingham.

**Stations Reopened – Yarm**

This Stockton-on-Tees station reopened in the 1990s. It is now served by the hourly weekday First TransPennine services between Middlesbrough, Leeds and Manchester Airport. On 16 April 2018, No. 185150 calls on a Middlesbrough-bound service.

On 18 April, a Grand Central Class 180 unit crosses the viaduct in the town. The original station was just to the north of the viaduct. Had it not closed in 1960, it would have undoubtedly appeared on the list of stations to be closed.